THE ULTIMATE

STEP-BY-STEP, EASY-TO-FOLLOW INSTRUCTIONS

HEBREW

TO MASTER THE ART OF READING IN **HEBREW**

READING GUIDE

WRITTEN BY
YAFIT KAMHAJI

THE ULTIMATE HEBREW READING GUIDE - Step-by-step, easy-to-follow instructions to master the art of reading in Hebrew.

FIRST EDITION

Don't miss the unique coloring books, picture and activity books that we have to offer. Visit amazon.com

INTRODUCTION

Welcome to The Ultimate Guide on how to read in Hebrew!

Learning to read Hebrew can seem daunting at first, especially if you're unfamiliar with the Hebrew alphabet and its unique script. However, with a bit of practice and dedication, you'll soon find yourself able to read and understand Hebrew texts with ease.

In this guide, we'll walk you through the basics of the Hebrew alphabet, including each letter's shape, name, and sound. We'll also cover the unique vowels system of the Hebrew language - the *Nikud*.

In this clear and simple guide you will also find common Hebrew words, as well as helpful tips and tricks for improving your reading skills and expand your Hebrew vocabulary.

Whether you're interested in reading Hebrew for religious or cultural reasons, or simply want to expand your language skills, this guide is the perfect place to start.

So, whether you're a complete beginner or have some prior knowledge of Hebrew, let's get started on this exciting journey of learning to read in Hebrew!

Here is an overview of everything you will learn in this guide. You can copy or cut out this page to have at hand while you are doing the exercises in this book or if you want to have it next to you while you practice reading.

The Alef Bet

Sound	Name	Shape		Sound	Name	Shape
M	Mem Sofit	ם		-	Alef	א
N	Nun	נ		B	Bet	בּ
N	Nun Sofit	ן		V	Vet	ב
S	Samej	ס		G	Gimel	ג
-	Ayin	ע		D	Dalet	ד
P	Pe	פּ		H	He	ה
F	Fe	פ		V	Vav	ו
F	Fe Sofit	ף		Z	Zayin	ז
TS	Tsadi	צ		CH	Chet	ח
TS	Tsadi Sofit	ץ		T	Tet	ט
K	Kuf	ק		Y	Yod	י
R	Reish	ר		K	Kaf	כּ
SH	Shin	שׁ		CH	Chaf	כ
S	Sin	שׂ		CH	Chaf Sofit	ך
T	Tav	ת		L	Lamed	ל
				M	Mem	מ

The Nikud

Sound	Name	Shape		Sound	Name	Shape
I	Chirik	●		A	Kamatz	ָ
I	Full Chirik	'		A	Patach	ַ
O	Cholan	●		A	Chataf Kamatz	ָ:
O	Full Cholam	ו		A	Chataf Patach	ַ:
U	Kubutz	●		E	Tzere	●●
U	Shuruk	ו		E	Segol	●●
-	Shva	●		E	Chataf Segol	●●●

I know you are eager to start your Hebrew learning journey, but first, there are some very important rules you should keep in mind in order to succeed in your study of reading Hebrew.

In Hebrew, reading starts from right to left.

Let's take the word "Shalom" which means peace and is also the traditional way of greeting in Hebrew.

שלום

4   3   2   1

In Hebrew, there are also printed and cursive letters.

Printed letters are generally used for official documents or letters, books, newspapers, etc.

Cursive letters are used for personal, handwritten notes and letters, diaries, etc.

Let's take the word Shalom again:

Print

Cursive

Printed and cursive letters should never be mixed in the same word or sentence.
The entire word must be written either in print or in cursive.

-3-

In Hebrew, there are no vowels.

What determines the sound each letter makes is a system of dots and lines that appear below or above each letter.

This system is called the "**NIKUD**."

When a child or adult starts to read Hebrew, all the words carry the *Nikud* to facilitate learning the language.
However, as they develop a deeper understanding of the Hebrew language, the *Nikud* is no longer used.

Official documents, books, publications, etc. do not include the *Nikud*.

-4-

The rules for the Nikud system are very complex.

The *Nikud* system in Hebrew can be quite challenging to master. It has a set of very complex rules that govern the placement and use of these marks.

For example, the same vowel mark may represent different sounds depending on its position relative to the consonants. Additionally, certain vowel sounds may be represented by multiple marks, making it difficult to determine which mark to use in a given situation. All of this can leave even the seasoned Hebrew readers scratching their heads in confusion.

Since this book is geared toward the beginner reader, we will try to simplify all the rules and learn the basics that will allow you to start reading simple words and sentences. However, you must be aware that every rule has an exception and we will not be able to cover every nuance of the *Nikud* system in this guide.

-5-

You will need A LOT of patience and practice!

While learning to read Hebrew is not impossible, it won't be mastered overnight.

Reading Hebrew requires a lot of practice.

Keep in mind that you need to get used to a different orientation and an unfamiliar alphabet. Adding the *Nikud* system to the mix can be very overwhelming.

Don't despair! You'll see that your reading fluency will improve gradually over time.
With perseverance and daily review,
I guarantee that you will see results.

-6-

English consonants and vowels and their Hebrew letters and Nikud equivalent.

In order to explain the sounds of Hebrew letters and *Nikud* symbols, I have used a comparison with the consonants and vowels of the English language.

Throughout this guide, I have used the English vowels A, E, I, O, and U to describe the sounds of different Hebrew letters and *Nikud* symbols. However, it is important to note that in English, the pronunciation of vowels can vary depending on their position in a word or the consonants that come before or after them. This can lead to confusion when using English vowels to describe the sounds of Hebrew letters and *Nikud* symbols.

To ensure accurate pronunciation, the vowels were used as follows:
- A as in the words: **a**pple, f**a**ther, etc.
- E as in the words: **e**gg, **e**l**e**phant, etc.
- I as in the words: **i**gloo, b**i**g, etc.
- O as in the words: **o**pen, c**o**ld, etc.
- U was used to represent the sound of a double O, as in the words z**oo**, b**oo**k, etc.

Here is an example of what you will find in this section:

Name of the
letter in Hebrew
and phonetics
→

Cursive form
→

BET -בֵּית

בּ

ב

← Print Form

The "*Bet*" sounds like the letter B.

Brief
explanation of
the sound
→

The "*Bet*" could make any of the following sounds depending on the *Nikud* under or above it:

בָ בֵ בִ בֹ בֻ
BU, BO, BI, BE, BA

When this letter appears at the beginning of a word, it always carries a dot.

Hebrew word
starting with that
letter and its
phonetics and
translation
←

בְּנָנָה
Ba-na-na
Banana

15

It's time to start!

The Hebrew Alphabet

ALEF - BET

Alef - אָלֶף

Ic א

The letter "*Alef*" is the first letter in the Hebrew Alphabet. It has a silent sound. It is not pronounced as a consonant letter, but takes on the sound of the *Nikud* under or above it.

The "*Alef*" could make any of the following sounds depending on the *Nikud* under or above it:

אֻ אֹ אִ אֶ אַ

U, O, I, E, A

אַבָּא

A-ba

Father

Bet בֵּית-

 בּ

The "*Bet*" sounds like the letter B.

The "*Bet*" could make any of the following sounds depending on the *Nikud* under or above it:

בֻּ בֹּ בִּ בֵּ בָּ

BU, BO, BI, BE, BA

When this letter appears at the beginning of a word, it always carries a dot.

בָּנָנָה

Ba-na-na

Banana

Vet בֵּית-

The "*Vet*" sounds like the letter V.

The "*Vet*" could make any of the following sounds depending on the *Nikud* under or above it:

בֻ בֹ בִ בֶ בָ

VU, VO, VI, VE, VA

Unlike the previous letter - בּ - the ב does not have a dot inside.

There are no words in Hebrew that begin with this letter. If this letter appears at the beginning of a word, it always carries a dot inside.

חָבֵר
Cha-ve-r
Friend

Gimel גִּימֶל-

ج ג

The "*Gimel*" sounds like the letter G (as in "great," "glee," and "good," rather than "general" or "gym.").

The "*Gimel*" could make any of the following sounds depending on the *Nikud* under or above it:

גֻ גֹ גִ גֶ גָ

GU, GO, GI, GE, GA

When the ג has an apostrophe on its top, left side - 'ג, it is pronounced as the letter "J" in English like in the word "Jeans".

When this letter appears at the beginning of a word, it always carries a dot.

Ge-ze-r

Carrot

Dalet -דָּלֶת

ד   ₹

The "*Dalet*" sounds like the letter D.

The "*Dalet*" could make any of the following sounds depending on the *Nikud* under or above it:

דָ דֵ דִ דֹ דֻ

DU, DO, DI, DE, DA

When this letter appears at the beginning of a word, it always carries a dot.

דֶּלֶת

De-le-t

Door

He - הֵא

The "*He*" sounds like a guttural "H" sound, similar to the sound at the beginning of the English word "house".

The "*He*" could make any of the following sounds depending on the *Nikud* under or above it:

הֻ הֵ הִ הֹ הָ הַ

HU, HO, HI, HE, HA

If this letter appears at the end of a word, it does not make a sound.

הַר
Ha-r
Mountain

Vav - וָו

ו /

The "*Vav*" sounds like the letter V.

The "*Vav*" could make any of the following sounds depending on the *Nikud* under or above it:

וֻ וֶ וִ וֹ וָ

VU, VO, VI, VE, VA

In the Hebrew language, the letter "*Vav*" is also used to represent the word "and". For example: Black and White - שחור וַלבן. The letter "*Vav*" will appear joined to the beginning of the second word.

Also, two "*Vav*" together - וו, make a sound equivalent to the English letter W like in the name Walter.

וֶרֶד

Ve-re-d

Rose

Zain - זַיִן

ז   *ʒ*

The "*Zain*" sounds like the letter Z.

The "*Zain*" could make any of the following sounds depending on the *Nikud* under or above it:

זָ   זֶ   זִ   זֹ   זֻ

ZU, ZO, ZI, ZE, ZA

זַמָר
Za-ma-r
Singer

Chet - חֵית

ח ח

The "*Chet*" has a guttural sound, similar to the "ch" in the Scottish pronunciation of the word "loch" or like the "J" in the Spanish pronunciation of the name "Juan". It is pronounced in the back of the throat, with a bit of a throat clearing sound.

The "*Chet*" could make any of the following sounds depending on the *Nikud* under or above it:

CHU, CHO, CHI, CHE, CHA

Cha-lo-n

Window

Tet - טֵית

ט

The "*Tet*" sounds like the letter T.

The "*Tet*" could make any of the following sounds depending on the *Nikud* under or above it:

טֻ טֶ טִ טֹ טַ
TU, TO, TI, TE, TA

טַבַּעַת
Ta-ba-at
Ring

Yod - יוֹד
ל ׳

The "*Yod*" sounds like the letter Y.

The "*Yod*" could make any of the following sounds depending on the *Nikud* under or above it:

ל ל ל ל ל

YU, YO, YI, YE, YA

יד
ya-d

Hand

Shall we take a short break to practice?

Here are a few exercises you can do:

- Go over the vocabulary words that appear at the bottom right corner of each page. Try to spot the letters you are already familiar with. Say out loud their name, their sound and what is their equivalent letter in English. While you go over the words, be extra careful to spot and correctly identify the ב and the כ.

- Match the list of the English vowels and consonants to their Hebrew equivalent.
  You can check your answers below.

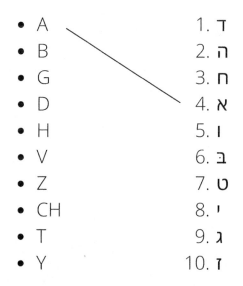

• A	1. ד
• B	2. ה
• G	3. ח
• D	4. א
• H	5. ו
• V	6. ב
• Z	7. ט
• CH	8. י
• T	9. ג
• Y	10. ז

A4, B3, G3, D7, H4, V5, Z2, CH6, T0, Y8

Kaf - כַּף

The "*Kaf*" sounds like the letter K.

The "*Kaf*" could make any of the following sounds depending on the *Nikud* under or above it:

כֻּ כֹ כִ כֵ כָ

KU, KO, KI, KE, KA

When this letter appears at the beginning of a word, it always carries a dot.

כֶּלֶב

Ke-le-v

Dog

Chaf - כָּף

כ
ך

The "*Chaf*" sounds like the Hebrew letter "Chet" - ח.
You can go back to page 22 to refresh your memory.

The "*Chaf*" could make any of the following sounds
depending on the *Nikud* under or above it:

כֻ   כֹ   כִ   כֶ   כַ

CHU, CHO, CHI, CHE, CHA

Unlike the previous letter - כ - the כ does not have a
dot inside.
There are no words in Hebrew that begin with this
letter. If this letter appears at the beginning of a word,
it always carries a dot.

מַסֵכָה

Ma-se-cha

Mask

Chaf Sofit - כֵּף סוֹפִית

The "*Chaf Sofit*" sounds the same as the previous letter "*Chaf*"- כ.

In Hebrew, the term "*Sofit*" means end or final. There are 5 *Sofit* letters in the Hebrew alphabet and they appear only at the end of the word.

In this case, when the last letter of a word is כ we change its written form and use the "*Chaf Sofit*" - ך. The sound, however, stays the same.
In other words, there will never be a word in Hebrew that ends with the letter כ. If this letter appears at the end of a word, it will always be in its "*Sofit*" form - ך.

The "*Chaf Sofit*" can make only 2 sounds depending on the *Nikud* besides it:

ךְ ךָ

CH, CHA

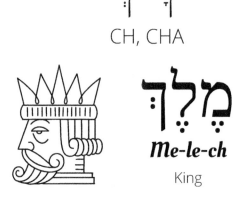

מֶלֶךְ

Me-le-ch

King

28

Lamed - לָמֶד
ל

The "*Lamed*" sounds like the letter L.

The "*Lamed*" could make any of the following sounds depending on the *Nikud* under or above it:

לֻ לֹ לִ לֶ לָ

LU, LO, LI, LE, LA

לִמוֹן

Li-mo-n

Lemon

Mem - מֶם

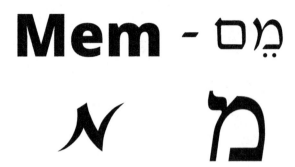

The "*Mem*" sounds like the letter M.

The "*Mem*" could make any of the following sounds depending on the *Nikud* under or above it:

מָ מֶ מִ מֹ מֻ

MU, MO, MI, ME, MA

מֶלַח

Me-la-ch

Salt

Mem Sofit - מֶם סוֹפִית

The "*Mem Sofit*" sounds the same as the previous letter "*Mem*"- **מ**.

Remember what we explained earlier about the "*Sofit*" letters? You can go back to page 28 to refresh your memory.

In this case, when the last letter of a word is **מ** we change its written form and use the "*Mem Sofit*" - **ם**. The sound, however, stays the same.

לֶחֶם

Le-che-m

Bread

Nun - נוּן

נ ﬦ

The "*Nun*" sounds like the letter N.

The "*Nun*" could make any of the following sounds depending on the *Nikud* under or above it:

נָ נֵ נִ נֹ נֻ

NU, NO, NI, NE, NA

נָמֵר

Na-me-r

Tiger

Nun Sofit - נוּן סוֹפִית

ן ׀

The "*Nun Sofit*" sounds the same as the previous letter "*Nun*"- נ.

Remember what we explained earlier about the "*Sofit*" letters? You can go back to page 28 to refresh your memory.

In this case, when the last letter of a word is נ we change its written form and use the "*Nun Sofit*" - ן. The sound, however, stays the same.

לֵיצָן

Ley-tsa-n

Clown

Shall we take a short break to practice?

Here are a few exercises you can do:

1. Go over the vocabulary words that appear at the bottom right corner of each page. Try to spot the letters you are already familiar with. Say out loud their name, their sound and what is their equivalent letter in English.

2. Carefully observe these very similar looking letters in Hebrew. Can you correctly identify them? What sound do they make?

בּ, בּ, כּ, כ

3. After familiarizing yourself with the concept of the "*Sofit*" letters, observe the following pairs of words. Circle the word that is spelled correctly.

- מלך / מלכ
- חמ / חם
- לימון / לימונ
- ברכ / ברך
- ימ / ים
- חמינ / חמין

It´s Trivia Time!

Answer the following questions:

1. What other letter in Hebrew makes the same sound as the בּ? _____
2. How many *Sofit* letters there are in the Hebrew alphabet? _____
3. Which Hebrew letter doesn't have a sound of its own and is dependent on the *Nikud* under it? _____
4. What other letter in Hebrew makes the same sound as the ח? _____
5. Which Hebrew letter is equivalent to the word "and"? _____
6. Which two Hebrew letters, from the one you have learned so far, will never appear in the beginning of a word? _____, _____
7. Which letter in Hebrew represents the sound of "ch"? _____

> How did you do?
> Don't be discouraged if you didn't get every answer correct the first time.
> Remember, becoming proficient in reading Hebrew takes practice and persistence.
>
> Keep going!

1. Vet, 2. Five, 3. Alef, 4. Chaf, 5. Vav, 6. Vet and Chaf, 7. Chet

Samech - סָמֶךְ
ס o

The "*Samech*" sounds like the letter S.

The "*Samech*" could make any of the following sounds depending on the *Nikud* under or above it:

סָ סֶ סִ סֹ סֻ
SU, SO, SI, SE, SA

סֵפֶר

Se-fe-r

Book

Ayin - עַיִן

עַ

The letter "*Ayin*" is very similar to the letter "*Alef*" as in, It is not pronounced as a separate letter, but takes on the sound of the *Nikud* under or above it.

However, the "*Ayin*" is pronounced as more of a guttural, throaty sound. It does not have an exact equivalent in English.

The "*Ayin*" could make any of the following sounds depending on the *Nikud* under or above it:

עֻ עֶ עִ עֹ עָ

U, O, I, E, A

עוּגָה

U-ga

Cake

Peh - פֵּא

The "*Peh*" sounds like the letter P.

The "*Peh*" could make any of the following sounds depending on the *Nikud* under or above it:

פָּ פֵּ פִּ פֹּ פֻּ

PU, PO, PI, PE, PA

When this letter appears at the beginning of a word, it always carries a dot.

פֶּרַח

Pe-ra-ch

Flower

Feh - פֵא

פ

The "*Feh*" sounds like the letter F.

The "*Feh*" could make any of the following sounds depending on the *Nikud* under or above it:

פָ פֵ פִ פֹ פֻ

FU, FO, FI, FE, FA

Unlike the previous letter - פּ - the פ does not have a dot inside.

There are no words in Hebrew that begin with this letter. If this letter appears at the beginning of a word, it always carries a dot.

רוֹפֵא

Ro-fe

Doctor

Feh Sofit - פֵא סוֹפִית

The "*Fe Sofit*" sounds the same as the previous letter "*Fe*"- פ.

Remember what we explained earlier about the "*Sofit*" letters? You can go back to page 28 to refresh your memory.

In this case, when the last letter of a word is פ we change its written form and use the "*Fe Sofit*" - ף. The sound, however, stays the same.

צֵדֶף

Tse-de-f

Seashell

Tsadi - צָדִי

צ

The "*Tsadi*" sounds like the combination of the letters "ts" as in the English word "Tsunami".

The "*Tsadi*" could make any of the following sounds depending on the *Nikud* under or above it:

צֻ צֹ צִ צֶ צָ

TSU, TSO, TSI, TSE, TSA

When this letter has an apostrophe on its top, left side - 'צ it will sound like the combination of letters "ch" as in the English words "chips", "check", etc.

צָב

Tsa-v

Turtle

Tsadi Sofit - צָדִי סוֹפִית

The "*Tsadi Sofit*" sounds the same as the previous letter "*Tsadi*"- צ.

Remember what we explained earlier about the "*Sofit*" letters? You can go back to page 28 to refresh your memory.

You can go back to page 28 to refresh your memory.

In this case, when the last letter of a word is צ we change its written form and use the "*Tsadi Sofit*" - ץ. The sound, however, stays the same.

Che-ts

Arrow

Shall we take a short break to practice?

Here are a few exercises you can do:

1. Go over the vocabulary words that appear at the bottom right corner of each page. Try to spot the letters you are already familiar with. Say out loud their name, their sound and what is their equivalent letter in English.

2. Match the list of the English vowels and consonants to their Hebrew equivalent.
   You can check your answers below.

• M	1. פ
• K	2. נ
• F	3. כ
• P	4. ס
• L	5. מ
• N	6. ל
• S	7. פ

3. After familiarizing yourself with the concept of the "*Sofit*" letters, observe the following pairs of words. Circle the word that is spelled correctly.

   • עץ / עצ
   • אפ / אף
   • מלפפון / מלפפונ
   • כריכ / כריך

Kuf - קוף

ק

The "*Kuf*" sounds like the letter K.

The "*Kuf*" could make any of the following sounds depending on the *Nikud* under or above it:

קֻ קֵ קִ קֹ קַ

KU, KO, KI, KE, KA

קֶשֶׁת

Ke-she-t

Rainbow

Reish - רֵישׁ

ר ׳

The "*Reish*" sounds like the letter R.

The "*Reish*" could make any of the following sounds depending on the *Nikud* under or above it:

רֻ רֶ רִ רֹ רָ

RU, RO, RI, RE, RA

רִמּוֹן

Ri-mo-n

Pomegranate

Shin - שִׁין

e שׁ

The "*Shin*" sounds like the combination of the letters SH.

The "*Shin*" could make any of the following sounds depending on the *Nikud* under or above it:

שֻׁ שׁוֹ שִׁ שֵׁ שֶׁ שָׁ

SHU, SHO, SHI, SHE, SHA

It is important to note that when the dot above the letter is on the right side, it is pronounced as "sh". When the dot above the letter is on the left side, it is pronounced as "s".
See the next letter for more information.

שֶׁמֶשׁ

She-me-sh

Sun

Sin - שִׂין

e   שׂ

The "*Sin*" sounds like the letter S.

Although the "*Shin*" and the "*Sin*" look exactly the same, you can differentiate between the two by noting the position of the dot above the letter.

If the dot is on the right side it is pronounced as the combination of the letters "sh", if the dot is on the left side, it is pronounced as the letter "s".

The "*Sin*" could make any of the following sounds depending on the *Nikud* under or above it:

שֻׂ שׂׂ שִׂ שֶׂ שָׂ

SU, SO, SI, SE, SA

שִׂמְלָה

Si-m-la

Dress

Tav - תָּו

The "*Tav*" sounds like the letter T.

The "*Tav*" could make any of the following sounds depending on the *Nikud* under or above it:

תָ תֵ תִ תֹ תֻ

TU, TO, TI, TE, TA

When this letter appears at the beginning of a word, it always carries a dot.

תַּנוּר

Ta-nu-r

Oven

It´s Trivia Time!

Answer the following questions:

1. In the Hebrew letter "*Shin*", is the dot on the top right or the top left of the letter? _____
2. What other letter in Hebrew makes the same sound as the ק? _____
3. What other letter in Hebrew makes the same sound as the ש? _____
4. What other letter in Hebrew makes the same sound as the ת? _____

Carefully observe these very similar looking letters in Hebrew. Can you correctly identify them? What sound do they make?

ד , ר

ה , ח , ת

CONGRATULATIONS!

You have finished learning all the letters in the Hebrew Alphabet!

Well done!

Remember that the key to being proficient in reading Hebrew is to practice, practice, practice. Keep going over the letters and familiarize yourself with their shape and sound. You will be surprised to realize that after a while you won't need to consult your book for the name and sound of the letters.

When you feel comfortable with your knowledge of the Hebrew Alphabet, continue to the next chapter of this book to learn about the **NIKUD** system.

The
NIKUD

Kamatz - קָמֶץ

The sound of the *Kamatz* is "a" as in the English word "**a**pple".

When this symbol appears under a letter, that letter assumes the sound "a".

For example, let's take the English word "land". The equivalent for the "la" sound in Hebrew would look like this:

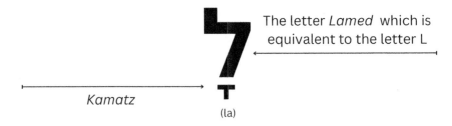

The letter *Lamed* which is equivalent to the letter L

Kamatz

(la)

Go back to page 8 and observe the word "*Shalom*". Can you spot the *Kamatz*?

Note: In some instances the *Kamatz*, when it appears at the beginning of a word, will sound like the Vowel "O". There are complex grammatical rules to spot those, but for the sake of the beginner learner we will not bring them up here. Any time a word like that will appear in this book it will be identified properly as to avoid confusion.

Patach - פַּתָח

The sound of the *Patach* is the same as the *Kamatz* - "a". When this symbol appears under a letter, that letter assumes the sound "a".

For example, let's take the Hebrew word for Banana, which sounds the same as in English. Observe the position of the *Patach* and *Kamatz* in this word. Remember, in Hebrew we start from right to left!

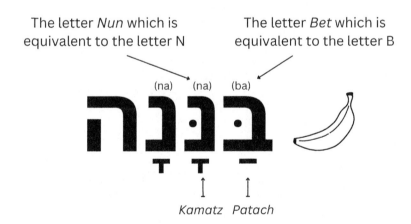

The letter *Nun* which is equivalent to the letter N

The letter *Bet* which is equivalent to the letter B

(na) (na) (ba)

בַּנָנָה

Kamatz Patach

The letter "*Bet*" with the *Patach* sounds like "ba". The letter "*Nun*" with the *Kamatz* sounds like "na".
Now you can read your first word in Hebrew.

Congratulations!

Shall we take a short break to practice?

Practice reading the following letters and words. Remember to start from right to left.

1. אָ, לָ, סָ, דַ, גַ, קָ
2. רָם, גַּג, סַל, יָד
3. אַבָּא, גַּבָּה
4. אַגָּדָה, מַתָּנָה

1. a, la, sa, da, ga, ka
2. ram, gag, sal, yad
3. aba, gaba
4. agada, matana

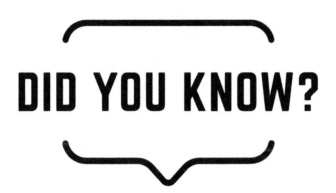

DID YOU KNOW?

It is estimated that approximately 9 million individuals speak Hebrew globally.

Israel is the primary country where Hebrew is predominantly spoken. 90% of Israelis are considered to be proficient speakers.

The second largest population of Hebrew speakers in the world is located in the United States.

Tsere - צֵירֵה

The sound of the *Tsere* is "e" as in the English word "**e**gg".

When this symbol appears under a letter, that letter assumes the sound "e".

For example, let's take the English word "leg". The equivalent for the "le" sound in Hebrew would look like this:

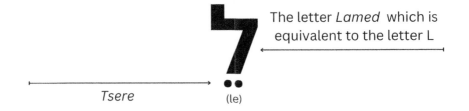

The letter *Lamed* which is equivalent to the letter L

Tsere

(le)

Segol - סֶגּוֹל

The sound of the *Segol* is the same as the *Tsere* - "e".
When this symbol appears under a letter, that letter assumes the sound "e".

For example, let's take the Hebrew word for "carrot". Observe the position of the *Segol* in this word. Can you try to read it?
Remember, in Hebrew we start from right to left!

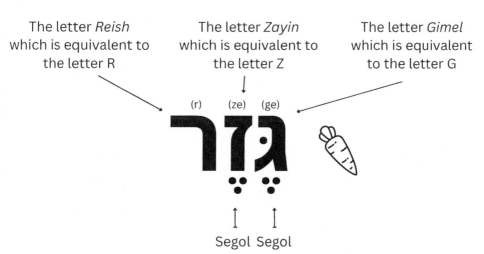

The letter *Reish* which is equivalent to the letter R	The letter *Zayin* which is equivalent to the letter Z	The letter *Gimel* which is equivalent to the letter G

(r)   (ze)   (ge)

גֶּזֶר

Segol Segol

The "*Gimel*" and "*Zayin*" with the *Segol* sound like "ge" and "ze" respectively. The letter "*Reish*" sounds like "R" and since it has no *Nikud* under it, it will maintain its simple sound "R".
Put everything together and you get the word - *Gezer* - carrot.

Shall we take a short break to practice?

Practice reading the following letters and words. Remember to start from right to left.

1. שָׁ, זֶ, וְ, יֵ, קֶ, צָ, תֵ

2. נֶס, זֵר, גַל, תֵל

3. בֶּגֶד, רֶגֶל, גֶּזֶר

4. מָלֵא, עָלֶה, נָמֵר

4. namer, aleh, male
3. gezer, regel, beged
2. tel, gal, zer, nes
1. te, tsa, ke, ya, ve, ze, sha

58

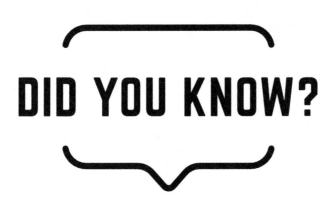

DID YOU KNOW?

During the Middle Ages, Hebrew served as the liturgical language of Judaism, primarily used for religious ceremonies and prayers.

However, it was not until the 19th century that efforts were made to revive Hebrew as a language for everyday use. A man by the name Eliezer Ben Yehuda played a key role in this revival and was the driving force behind the development of Modern Hebrew as the standardized form of the language.

In essence, Hebrew transitioned from being solely a language for religious worship during the Middle Ages to becoming a language for daily communication in modern times.

Chirik - חִירִיק

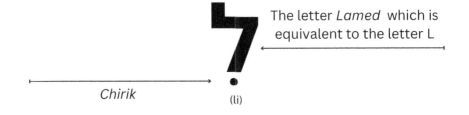

The sound of the *Chirik* is "i" as in the English word "**i**gloo".

When this symbol appears under a letter, that letter assumes the sound "i".

For example, let's take the English word "little". The equivalent for the "li" sound in Hebrew would look like this:

The letter *Lamed* which is equivalent to the letter L

Chirik

(li)

Full Chirik - חִירִיק מלא

The sound of the *Full Chirik* is the same as the sound of the normal *Chirik* - "i".

In some cases, the Hebrew letter "*Yod*" - **י** may appear after a letter to also denote the sound of "i". In the visual representation above, the dotted square was used to represent any given letter in the Hebrew alphabet.

For example, let's take the Hebrew word "*Limudim*" which means studies. Observe both the *Chirik* in this word.

לִמוּדִים

(m) (di) (mu) (li)

↑ ↑
Full   Chirik
Chirik

All of the above is relevant only when there is no other *Nikud* in the letter or in the letter "*Yod*" - **י**.

More on this on the next page...

Let us observe the following examples:

מַיִם

Even though in this word there is a letter followed by a "Yod" - י, it is important to understand that this is not a Chirik. In this case, the letter "Mem" - מ has a "Patach" and it should be read es "ma". The letter "Yod" - י has a "Chirik" which should be read as "yi". Together the whole word should be read - "ma-yi-m" which means water.

בֵּיצָה

Even though in this word there is a letter followed by a "Yod" - י, it is important to understand that this is not a "Chirik". In this case, the letter "Bet" - ב has a "Tsere" and should be read as "be". The letter "Yod" - י has no Nikud which means it should be read as its pure form "y". Together the whole word should be read as - "bey-tsa" which means egg.

Shall we take a short break to practice?

Practice reading the following letters and words. Remember to start from right to left.

1. שֶׁ, כְּ, סֶ, בַּ, טִי, רָ

2. חַג, עִם, קִיר, גֶּר

3. שִׁירָה, חָבִית, יָפֶה

4. בֵּיצָה, לֵיצָן, נָשִׁים

Cholam - חֹלָם

●

The sound of the *Cholam* is "o" as in the English word "**o**range".

When this symbol appears on the top left corner of a letter, that letter assumes the sound "o".

For example, let's take the English word "low". The equivalent for the "lo" sound in Hebrew would look like this:

Cholam ⟶ •ל The letter *Lamed* which is equivalent to the letter L ⟵

(lo)

Full Cholam - חוֹלָם מלא

וֹ

The sound of the *Full Cholam* is the same as the sound of the normal *Cholam* - "o".

In some cases, the Hebrew letter "*Vav*" - ו, with a dot on top may appear after a letter to also denote the sound of "o". In the visual representation above, a dotted square was used to represent any given letter in the Hebrew alphabet.

For example, lets take the word "*Rofe*" which means doctor:

רוֹפֵא

(fe) (ro)

↑

Full Cholam

It is important to note that when a word is written without any *Nikud* like in official publications, books and documents, the *Full Cholam* will be used. However, in some cases where the word is written with *Nikud*, a regular *Cholam* might appear.
For example:

שחור

(r) (cho)(sha)

↑

If the word is written without any *Nikud*, a *Full Cholam* is used to help with the pronunciation.

שְׁחֹר

(r)(cho) (sha)

↑

If the whole word is written with *Nikud*, a *Cholam* might be enough to read the word.

65

Shall we take a short break to practice?

Practice reading the following letters and words. Remember to start from right to left.

1. לָ, תֶּ, רִ, אֹ, גַ, זוֹ

2. דֹב, גוֹל, עַז, יוֹם

3. מֶלוֹן, שָׁלוֹם, מוֹרָה

4. כָּחֹל, שׁוֹשַׁנָּה

1. la, te, ri, o, ga, zo
2. dov, gol, az, yom
3. melon, shalom, mora
4. kachol, shoshana

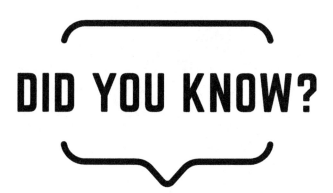

DID YOU KNOW?

Hebrew is one of the languages that is regulated by an official academy.

The Academy of the Hebrew Language, which was founded by the Israeli government in 1953, serves as the language's regulatory authority. Like other official academies around the world, it provides guidance on grammar and vocabulary selection, ensuring the preservation and development of the language for future generations.

Kubutz - קִבּוּץ

The sound of the *Kubutz* is "oo" as in the English word "z**oo**". For the sake of this book, we will represent that sound with the letter U.

When this symbol appears under a letter, that letter assumes the sound "u".

For example, let's take the English word "Book". The equivalent for the "boo" sound in Hebrew would look like this:

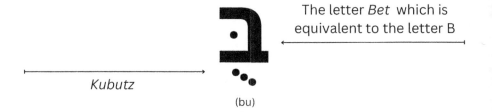

The letter *Bet* which is equivalent to the letter B

Kubutz

(bu)

Shuruk - שׁוּרוּק

The sound of the *Shuruk* is the same as the sound of the *Kubutz* - "u".

In some cases, the Hebrew letter "*Vav*" - ו, with a dot inside may appear after a letter to also denote the sound of "u". In the visual representation above, a dotted square was used to represent any given letter in the Hebrew alphabet.

For example, lets take the word "*Sus*" which means horse:

(s)   (su)

↑
Shuruk

It is important to note that when a word is written without any *Nikud* like in official publications, books and documents, the "*Shuruk*" will be used. However, in some cases where the word is written with *Nikud*, a "*Kubutz*" might appear.
For example:

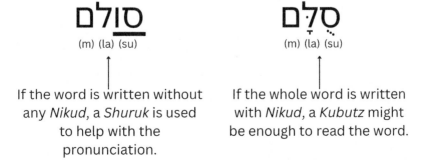

סוּלם	סֻלָּם
(m) (la) (su)	(m) (la) (su)
↑	↑
If the word is written without any *Nikud*, a *Shuruk* is used to help with the pronunciation.	If the whole word is written with *Nikud*, a *Kubutz* might be enough to read the word.

Shall we take a short break to practice?

Practice reading the following letters and words. Remember to start from right to left.

1. בֶּ יְ הַ ה טְ טֹ חוֹ גֹ גֵ וֶ

2. דּוֹד, בּוּל, תּוּת

3. סֻלָּם, חָשׁוּב, שׁוּרָה

4. שֻׁלְחָן, טֶלֶפוֹן

DID YOU KNOW?

In the study of the Hebrew Bible and Jewish mysticism, each letter in the Hebrew alphabet is assigned a specific numerical value. This numerical system is called "*Gematria*" and is used to uncover hidden meanings and connections between words and phrases. By calculating the numerical value of a word or phrase, it is possible to gain deeper insights into its spiritual and mystical significance.

Here is a table of the Hebrew letters and their numerical value:

Letter	Numerical Value	Letter	Numerical Value
א	1	ל	30
ב	2	מ	40
ג	3	נ	50
ד	4	ס	60
ה	5	ע	70
ו	6	פ	80
ז	7	צ	90
ח	8	ק	100
ט	9	ר	200
י	10	ש	300
כ	20	ת	400

For example, the Hebrew word for "life" - חי (*chai*) has a numerical value of 18. The letter "*Chet*" equals 8 and the letter "Yod" equals 10. it is common for Jewish people to give gifts or donations in multiples of 18 as a way of wishing someone a long and healthy life.

Shva - שווא

The "*Shva*" symbol is a little different from the other symbols. It represents the pure sound of a consonant letter without any vowels.

Let's take the following letters:
B, D, F, K, L, M, N, P, R, S, T
Can you try and sound them without any vowels?

Observe the following English words and note the bold letters: **b**rave, ha**r**d, boo**k**, wi**n**dow. Can you try and sound them alone?

Now let's see how they would be represented in Hebrew:

Brave   בְּ   (the letter ב sounds like the letter B)

Ha**r**d   רְ   (the letter ר sounds like the letter R)

Boo**k**   קְ   (the letter ק sounds like the letter K)

Wi**n**dow   נְ   (the letter נ sounds like the letter N)

Note: There are a few cases when the "*Shva*" will actually sound like the sound "e". In the next page we will explain the two most important cases.

Shva - שווא

When the "*Shva*" appears in the beginning of a word, in most cases it will sound like the vowel "e".
For example, observe the Hebrew word "leat" which means slow.

(t) (a) (le)

Because the *Shva* is in the beginning of a word, it sounds like "le" instead of just "l".

When there are two letters with "*Shva*" one after the other, the first letter with "*Shva*" will sound like a normal "*Shva*" and the second letter will sound like the vowel "e".
This is a less common occurrence and does not happen in daily Hebrew words. For that reason, we will not dwell more on this subject.

There are a few more less common *Nikud* symbols which are important to note:

Chataf Kamatz - חֲטַף קָמָץ

 Makes the sound "a"

Chataf Patach - חֲטַף פַּתָּח

 Makes the sound "a"

Chataf Segol - חֲטַף סֶגּוֹל

 Makes the sound "e"

Shall we take a short break to practice?

This time we are going to change things up a little bit.

On the right side you will find a list containing words in English, written with Hebrew letters and *Nikud*. Can you try and match them to the English words on the left? Remember to start from right to left.

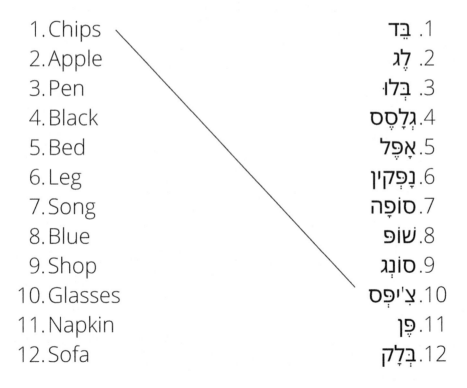

1. Chips	בֵּד .1
2. Apple	לֶג .2
3. Pen	בְּלוּ .3
4. Black	גְלָסֶס.4
5. Bed	אָפֵּל.5
6. Leg	נָפְקִין.6
7. Song	סוֹפָה.7
8. Blue	שׁוֹפּ.8
9. Shop	סוֹנְג.9
10. Glasses	צִ'יפְּס.10
11. Napkin	פֶּן.11
12. Sofa	בְּלֶק.12

Here are a few additional rules that are important to know about the *NIKUD*

- **No *Nikud* in a letter.** When a letter does not have any *Nikud* under or above it, it will be read as it's pure consonant sound.

- **Text without *Nikud*.** As we explained in the beginning of this guide (page 8), newspapers, books, official documents, etc. do not use the *Nikud*. Let's take the word כַּדוּר which means ball in Hebrew and we will look at it without any *Nikud*:

כדור

If you are a complete beginner and you are faced with this word, most likely you will not be able to read it. Do not worry! As you practice reading and you amplify your Hebrew vocabulary, you will come to understand that when these four letters come in that precise order, it means "*Ka-du-r*" - ball. That is why learning vocabulary and visualizing each word is key to improving your reading skill.

- **Same letters, different *Nikud*.** Sometimes two words can have the exact same letters but different *Nikud*:

סֵפֶר / סַפָּר

The word on the right is read "*Sapar*" and it means "barber" and the word on the left is read "*Sefer*" which means "book". However, without any *Nikud* both of these words look the same: **ספר**.

When you are faced with a word like this without *Nikud* and you are not sure how it should be read, you need to try to infer it from the context of the text you are reading. If you are reading an article about grooming, most likely the word is "*Sapar*" which means "barber", however, if you are reading a literature text, most likely the word is "*Sefer*" which means "book".

- **"*Chet*" with "*Patach*".** When a word ends with the letter "*Chet*" - ח with the *Nikud* symbol of "*Patach*" under it - חַ, it is read as "ach" instead of "cha". Observe the following words and the correct way to read them:
  - תַפּוּחַ (apple) - is read "ta-pu-a-ch" instead of "ta-pu-cha"
  - יָרֵחַ (moon) - is read "ya-re-a-ch" instead of "ya-re-cha".

- **_Dagesh._** Sometimes you will spot dots inside letters without any apparent reason. We know already that the letters בג,ד,כ,פ,ת at the beginning of a word should always carry a dot inside. Also the dot is important to differentiate between the letters בּ-ב, כּ-כ, פּ-פ. Aside from these cases, any other dot you spot inside a letter is called a "_Dagesh_" which is translated as emphasis. It is used sometimes to indicate where the stress of the word should be. Lets observe again the word כַּדּור. Can you see the dot in the letter ד? That dot is there to indicate that the ד should be read with a bit more force.

The use of the "_Dagesh_" can sometimes be tricky because not all Hebrew letters can take a "_Dagesh_", and there are certain rules that govern when a "_Dagesh_" should be used. Since this is a guide for beginners we will not go deeper into this subject but it is important for you to understand the concept of the "_Dagesh_" so you don't get confused when you see some dots inside letters.

Reading Practice

in the next two pages you will find a list of 40 common words in Hebrew, together with their phonetics and translation.

Cover the phonetics column and try to read the Hebrew word before you look at the phonetics.

If you didn't get a word right, don't be discouraged. Try to take note of your mistake and learn from that how to improve your reading.

Translation	Phonetics	Word
maybe	u-la-y	אוּלַי
where	e-i-fo	אֵיפֹה
food	o-che-l	אֹכֶל
mother	i-ma	אִמָּא
country	e-re-ts	אֶרֶץ
yesterday	e-t-mo-l	אֶתְמוֹל
stomach	be-te-n	בֶּטֶן
home	ba-i-t	בַּיִת
morning	bo-ke-r	בֹּקֶר
big	ga-do-l	גָּדוֹל
paper	da-f	דַּף
cat	cha-tu-l	חָתוּל
day	yo-m	יוֹם
boy	ye-le-d	יֶלֶד
dog	ke-le-v	כֶּלֶב
yes	ke-n	כֵּן
chair	ki-se	כִּסֵּא
no	lo	לֹא
white	la-va-n	לָבָן
night	la-i-la	לַיְלָה

Translation	Phonetics	Word
tomorrow	ma-cha-r	מָחָר
computer	ma-ch-she-v	מַחְשֵׁב
water	ma-i-m	מַיִם
car	me-cho-ni-t	מְכוֹנִית
dangerous	me-su-ka-n	מְסֻכָּן
family	mi-sh-pa-cha	מִשְׁפָּחָה
candle	ne-r	נֵר
work	a-vo-da	עֲבוֹדָה
pen	e-t	עֵט
city	i-r	עִיר
tree	e-ts	עֵץ
flower	pe-ra-ch	פֶּרַח
small	ka-ta-n	קָטָן
head	ro-sh	רֹאשׁ
street	re-cho-v	רְחוֹב
black	sha-cho-r	שָׁחֹר
table	shu-l-cha-n	שֻׁלְחָן
hour	sha-a	שָׁעָה
restroom	she-ru-ti-m	שֵׁרוּתִים
apple	ta-pu-a-ch	תַּפּוּחַ

What is the next step?

You have worked hard and you are on the right track to mastering th skill of reading in Hebrew. Remember it is a process and every ste you take will get you closer to being a proficient reader.

Here are a few suggestions on how to continue from this point.

- **Practice.** If possible, try to dedicate time every day to go over th guide and read it again and again. Visualize the form of the letter and the *Nikud* symbols and memorize their sound. Read all th vocabulary words in the letter pages and in the exercises.

- **Expand your Hebrew vocabulary.** The more vocabulary yc learn the better you learn to identify words and your reading sk will improve. The internet is a treasure trove of material you ca use. There are websites, YouTube channels, books and e-book dedicated to learning Hebrew. Try to take advantage of all that available.

- **Learn to write the Hebrew letters.** Start with mastering th cursive writing since most likely that is the type of writing you w use more frequently. Remember that in Hebrew, handwriting done with the cursive letters. There are many resources and book online that will help you learn the correct way to trace each letter.

- **Start reading short texts.** Children's books are a great way t start your Hebrew reading journey. They are clear and simple an offer basic vocabulary words you can learn along the way.

- **Enlist the help of a friend.** If you have a Hebrew speaking frier or someone you are familiar with that can help you, don't hesita to ask them to listen to you read, and correct you if necessary.

כֹּל הַכָּבוֹד!

Ko-l   ha-ka-vo-d

Well done!

NOW AVAILABLE BY YAFIT KAMHAJI

The Complete
Alef - Bet
Activity Book

Alef - Bet
Writing
Workbook -
Print

Alef - Bet Writing
Workbook -
Cursive

My First
Hebrew Words
- Fruits and
Vegetables

My First Hebrew
Words - Food

First Hebrew Words
Alef - Bet

My First 100
Hebrew Words

Printed in Great Britain
by Amazon

26042648R00051